Learn a Southern Drawl

by Ivan Borodin

Introduction

There is magic in the Southern Drawl. It has the power to envelope the listeners in a bath of honey, and to fit as snug as broken-in blue jeans.

There are things you can get away with in this world, and things you can't–like a bad Southern accent.

Facing your harshest critics (such as directors, casting directors, teachers, or even yourself), there's no reason to feel defeated.

Straighten those shoulders, settle your jangled nerves, and embrace this genuine opportunity.

Digest this material, as well as the free YouTube videos that support it, and you'll soon be possessed not by fear, but by your performance, the journey, and the moment itself.

1

Intrusive 'Uh' Before Key Vowels

A noticeable 'uh' sound appears before 'ee',
'A', 'O' and 'U'. This slight 'uh' must be
added quickly.

2

Long E becomes UH-EE

teenage, feels, weave, really, we

The *beaches* were hot, and *he* was miserable in the *heat*.

Leave everything else to *Peter*.

Steve kept photos of *me* in a *beat* up wallet close to his heart.

I *realized* I must *teach* the world to *deal* with *evil*.

Sheila marched to the *beat* of a different drum.

I'm tired of you *treating* everyone on this *team* like pawns.

I assure you I am more than *equal* to the task.

This is a side of you I haven't *seen* before.

The *league* has enough to *deal* with.

3

That would *squeeze* the life out of *me.*

You don't have to *repeat* yourself.

Why don't you give this *wheelchair* to someone who *needs* it?

The ad was a tantalizing *tease.*

He found himself *knee-deep* in swamp water.

4

Long A becomes UH-A

The Standard American speaker pronounces this 'A' vowel with a very clear sound, free of any preceding half-vowels. The Southerner starts the vowel with an initial darkening.

insane, base, regulations, weight, amazing

On any given *day*, the person I love best depends on what *place* in my heart needs to be *saved.*

Have you no *shame?*

I'll *make* it worth your while.

Everyone should get out of the *way.*

I was *amazed* to spot a *spaceship.*

The three-point *play* was the result of getting fouled on a corkscrew *lay up* at the end of the *game*.

The *plane* can't *take* that kind of *strain*.

The *mayor saved* the *agency*.

The *space* between my ears is a *dangerous neighborhood*.

He *gave* it to you, and he can *take* it *away*.

I'm digging through the trash in search of your *reputation*.

It's *taking* all my *concentration* to *stay* in this *conversation*.

Are you *saying* that you're willing to *trade*?

The *breaking* news was setting Twitter *ablaze* with *praise*.

Maybe this *situation* is too *dangerous* for us at this *stage*.

Take this along in *case* she *faints*.

6

The Long O becomes uh-O

Southern folk know the value of taking their sweet time, so when they pronounce the long O, they add a slight 'uh' sound at the beginning of the vowel.

gold, robot, own, poem, phony, open, polar

I still *vote "no"*.

She *hoped* that *Joseph* understood the concept of boundaries.

Leave a message at the *tone*.

We *only* want to help you before you hurt yourself.

There are stories that need telling that never get *told*, because *folks* can't bear to hear them.

His economy of language made him quite *well-spoken*.

The entire city was *thrown* into racial unrest.

Those disgruntled *folks* were *only* fighting for their *homes.*

They didn't *know* the police were just putting on a *show.*

I had to work to *control* the *tone* of my voice.

They represent something *noble.*

I *owe* you for the other day.

Some of you *don't know* each other.

He is a dominating presence that likes to use his hands on his *opponents.*

Is there a *phone* book in here?

I *woke* up and remembered the *whole* story.

That didn't *go over so* well.

The Long U becomes uh-U

Manipulate the vowel so that a short 'uh'
sound precedes the long U.

stupid, truth, Eugene, assume, knew

Did you *do* this to yourself on purpose?

It's been almost *two* years.

I've been *doing* some soul searching.

The expensive *suit* came with tailored *shoes*.

Voodoo was practiced in the *moonlight*.

The *newbie* finally gets a *clue*.

I *usually* leave that for the cleanup *crew*.

I don't like this *community* getting caught in
the cross-hairs.

I met him in a *Buddhist* bookstore.

9

This delicate change needs to be performed in a subtle manner. Pulling it off will make the speaker appear to transform before the listener's eyes.

We interrupt to bring *you* an emergency *news* break.

Is it *too* late for tryouts?

Who decided it was *cool* for *you* to *use* that?

She sat cross-legged on the bed in her *room*.

The team *moved* within a breath of the playoffs.

You *deserve* to be rewarded.

That is the *root* of my enduring faith.

I hate crying, because it *ruins* all chances of winning an argument.

She wore a *cute tube* top.

10

The Reduction of Certain Sounds

The South is famous for the reduction of the 'I' and 'OY' sounds. These changes grow out of the fact that the Southern drawl is generated higher and further back in the face than the standard American accent.

The Long I changes to 'Aa-ee'

In the standard American accent, the long I begins with the short O (as in *honest*), then completes itself with a long E (as in *key*). Southern speakers begin the long I with a short A (as in *cat*).

12

Here's an exercise to help clarify how the long I is pronounced in the South. A word featuring the short A will precede a word with a long I, followed by a sentence that will reinforce the change.

laugh, life: You're a *life-saver,* mister.

sad, side: I dove onto the linoleum and landed on my *side*.

tap, type: How could you *type* that into a book for all the world to see?

You almost can't go too far with this sound. When I was in Plano, Texas in '96, I heard my name spoken a hundred times, and it always had a twangy bite to it.

13

island, psychic, quite, decide, hide

For the longest *time*, I thought you were the *guy's wife.*

Why did you believe we could form an *alliance?*

I am no longer permitted access to such *files.*

It's *unlikely* that he's just being *kind.*

How *nice* of you to ask!

He gripped the pistol in his *right* hand.

Are you *trying* to read *my mind?*

They wanted to *invite* us in person.

The *flight* was delayed.

The *guy* was *right* to crush that *spider.*

That's the only *skyscraper* with a heliport.

OY reduces to AW

This change sounds like the vowel has to

suck in its gut in order to slip through a

sideways grin.

point, void, joint, poison, toy, soy

She met with the dapper *lawyer* over sweet
tea and pecan pie.

You have the *choice* of doing this now or
later.

Should I use the toaster or the *broiler*?

One must be either very young or very
hungry to *enjoy* its flavor.

What was that *noise*?

Behind the tinny *voice* on the cell phone, I
could make out the sounds of crickets
chirping.

15

The Nasality of the Southern Drawl

Southern speakers originate their sound higher in the face and further back in the mouth than speakers of standard American English. This makes the Southern drawl a predominantly nasal accent. A lot of sound comes through the nose, and this is demonstrated on the following sounds.

Clip the Short U

Employ the nasal cavity when producing this sound.

touch, much, above, us, nothing, justice

You shouldn't *rush* getting to know people.

A bit of iron *tucked* into your belt might make you feel more secure.

Cut the lights and follow at a safe distance.

Look *up* the word sometime.

She was attracted to a *knuckle*-dragging, testesterone-laden, neanderthal beast.

I'm *done wondering* what to *become*.

It's not for me to *judge*.

My first *husband* was quite the *punster*.

I feel like I've been living in a *bubble*.

Distort the Short I

The Southerner clouds the pronunciation of this vowel.

women, did, sitting, simply, window

Her *lipstick* matched the *ribbon* in her hair.

In an *instant,* much of Atlanta's *brilliant* skyline became a gloomy shadow againt the night sky.

You shouldn't have *criticized* her *singing.*

He *slid* behind me and grabbed my *wrist.*

Give the *kid* the gun that *killed* his *twin.*

Why don't you put a *lid* on it?

I asked her to *sit* somewhere in the *living* room.

He was a *pretty interesting* person.

'OU' as in 'OUT' picks up an 'EAH' sound before it

Southern accents are frequently described as warm and buttery, but this diphthong comes packed with a nasal scratchiness.

power, mountains, around, outside

Try to draw him away from the *crowd.*

Can we edit that *out* later?

It's one of those moments you're not *proud* of.

I'm learning *how* to live with the strange currents that flow through me.

That *sounds* exciting.

Her dying request was that I plant a *flower* beside her grave.

19

The AW of 'Drawl'

The Southern drawl can be described as a shaking in pitch as a word is uttered–a sort of tremolo. This shake is heard throughout the accent, but it can really be distinguished on the AW sound.

along, coffee, hawk, call, always

I never figured out how you *draw all* those lines.

He *walked* over to stand against the *wall*.

The *office* had *frosted*-glass windows.

You probably have to *talk* with him yourself.

I just found out that it's *falling* apart.

The Short A shiver

This sound picks up a medial 'Y'. A word like 'cat' will wind up sounding like 'ca-yat'. Be sure to measure up with the smooth tone that Southerners produce, like warm molasses on homemade ice cream.

after, ask, matter, jacket, hadn't

Do y'all consider the runner *adequate, average,* or *fast?*

The *manner* in which he *inhaled* was *rather dramatic.*

I wouldn't let her *pat* me down.

Did I hear you whistling Merle *Haggard back* there in the warehouse?

That made my nightmares seem like a *happy* place.

Bite the Hard R

When R appears at the end of a word, the modern Southern speaker over-pronounces it and makes it nasal.

frontier, margarita, nearly, bar, served

Marcus has some *serious cardiac* problems.

I'd *prefer* that you be *encouraging.*

I don't *normally* do house calls, but I'll be there *tomorrow.*

Do you know *where* the *cigar* smoke is coming from?

He *turned* and *started* out the *door.*

Georgia can be a *scary* place.

Arthur stood on the *stairs* with the other *workers.*

Southern Grammar

In may other languages, there are two ways to say 'You'–'you' as a person and 'you' as a group. When a typical American speaker says 'you', he can mean either case.

In recent times, 'you people' or 'you guys' (even when addressing women) has become the norm for Americans when speaking to a group. Other appropriate forms include 'All of you', 'most of you' and 'some of you'.

The Southerner wraps all these possibilities into one blanket expression–*y'all*.

23

Y'all come back now, y'hear?

What can I do for *y'all*?

Southerners will even use it when speaking to a single person:

Hey, Bubba, what *y'all* need?

By the way, can you guess the plural of 'y'all'?

All y'all.

I was speaking to *all y'all* about it yesterday.

24

Southerners don't 'plan' to do anything.

They say they are 'fixin' to do something.

I'm *fixin* to repair that roof.

I'm *fixin* on getting me some chicken pot pie.

25

Final Notes

Have you ever studied children's behavior? When they complete a task, they scream in glee and jump into each other's arms. It doesn't matter to them if they skin their knees. They just will their way through, taking challenges head-on. They aren't beholden to rules of perfection. It is with such childlike joy that accents should be practiced.

The adult actor needs to discard any feelings of resentment and display his pearly whites, remembering that performing dialects is a seemingly magical gift. Pronounce a vowel just the right way, and the listener is transported back to a memory–or awestruck by the transformation.

So have fun. Review the material as much as you need, but do so with a sense of play.

The author intends to make support for this publication available online. At the time of this writing, YouTube is the most popular site for posting videos that demonstrate chapters of this book.

27

To find online lessons, search **IvanBorodin**
and/or **Learn a Southern Drawl** on
YouTube.

The author recognizes the Internet as an
evolving beast. Should another site become
the leader in social media, please search for
support for this book using the tags listed
above.

28

Sources for Future Study

Film: *Mud, Cape Fear, Gone with the Wind, Crazy Heart, Raising Arizona, No Country for Old Men, Junebug, Tender Mercies, Driving Miss Daisy, The Fifth Element, Natural Born Killers, Steel Magnolias, Wild at Heart, Places in the Heart, The Help, Walk the Line*

Television: *Justified, Reba, In the Heat of the Night*

About the Author

I grew up in New York City, but my father had lived in the South, and bought property in Myrtle Beach where we summered.

Most New Yorkers consider Southern ways as boring as staring at airplane TV with the sound off, but I was invited to see Johnny Cash perform at a State fair–and became hooked on Country music. Its sense of irony, respect for family, and appreciation of salt-water-taffy sunsets became my first guilty pleasure.

By the time I was a teenager, I spoke three languages: English, New York, and Southern. You might say I became a speech coach as a crime of opportunity. The first accent I taught when I began teaching at City College was predictably a drawl.

When I'm not acting or teaching, I spend a great deal of time writing the *Pandora* novels, an epic horror-suspense series which I placed dab-smack in South Carolina. Writing thrillers gives me a chance to practice my three native tongues.

I continue to teach privately, both from my studio in Hollywood and via Skype worldwide.

Ivan Borodin

1626 N. Wilcox Avenue #490

Los Angeles, California 90028

IvanPresents@gmail.com

home (323) 319-4826

Skype handle: IvanBorodinUSA

Made in the USA
San Bernardino, CA
25 March 2015